He Put A New Song
In My Mouth

He Put A New Song In My Mouth

Revelation of prophetic songs for the church

Rob & Vicki Parks

authorHOUSE®

AuthorHouse™ LLC
1663 Liberty Drive
Bloomington, IN 47403
www.authorhouse.com
Phone: 1-800-839-8640

Published by AuthorHouse   10/22/2013

ISBN: 978-1-4918-2871-7 (sc)
ISBN: 978-1-4918-2872-4 (e)

Library of Congress Control Number: 2013919068

Contents

➤ FOREWORD ⬅

Ephesians 5: 31 NAS "FOR THIS REASON A MAN SHALL LEAVE HIS FATHER AND MOTHER AND SHALL BE JOINED TO HIS WIFE, AND THE TWO SHALL BECOME ONE FLESH. 32 This mystery is great; but I am speaking with reference to Christ and the church. 33 Nevertheless, each individual among you also is to love his own wife even as himself, and the wife must *see to it* that she respects her husband."

This may appear to be a strange way to have begun a foreword but nonetheless this verse of Scripture reveals to me what I have seen in the lives of Rob and Vicki Parks. The way I understand this verse of Scripture is that a believing wife is to be supportive and a helpmate to her believing husband in carrying out and fulfilling the work allotted to him by the Heavenly Father, just as it is with the church, as a helpmate to Jesus in carrying out the work allotted to Him by the Heavenly Father, in His ongoing life in the world today.

In the some 40 years that I have known and watched the lives of Rob and Vicki I have seen the oneness as was prayed for by Jesus, for the church in the Gospel of John 17:22 "--that they be one, just as we are one.--".

Their diligence to serve the Lord had, at times, caused them to move too swiftly, but nevertheless their willingness to move at His call, no matter the cost, has always turned out to be a spiritual reward in their lives. As I said once before, I've always seen Rob as a man on the run, unknown by me and possibly by Rob himself at the time, running from the traditions of man, but none the less ever seeking the path laid out for him by the Lord. I believe Rob has never been quite able to escape being faced with the traditions of man (Mark 7:13) because he is as one crying out in the wilderness, where so many of the well meaning believers are living today, trapped in the traditions of man with a deep desire in their hearts to be set free. The prophetic side of Rob is that he is a visionary but never losing sight of those who are somewhat nearsighted and unwilling to step out when the call of the Lord comes.

On the other hand Rob's wife Vicki, being more or less a counter weight in their lives together, was a bulwark of steadfastness, faithfulness and respect for Rob and the call God has placed on his life. Without a doubt Vicki was the woman spoken of in Proverbs 31:10-31 **"an excellent wife"** and truly an anointed worshiper and worship leader, writing many of her worship songs herself. Often times people see worship only in verbal song, music and praise. True worship is being in harmony with the Father's will for the moment, no matter what the task or activities at hand may be, that was Vicki's life no matter where she was, in a church setting, in the workplace or one-on-one with others, her life, in whatever mode excelled in worship.

The passages in this book give us wise direction and insight for our lives in Christ Jesus, as well as a brief testimony of Rob and Vickie's journey toward maturity in Christ. Rob is still on the run, moving and having his being in the Lord. Vicki has moved on in her journey, leaving a legacy of true harmony and an example to women of a true helpmate in Christ Jesus. **Vickie Lynn Parks – June 24th, 1954 - August 23rd, 2013**

Charlie R. Richards
Friend and pastor

➤ Introduction ◄

This book chronicles my wife, Vicki, and I's journey through life and the kingdom. It incorporates many truths that God has revealed to us along the way. In chapter 15, it's stated, "our lifes aren't a fifty yard dash but a marathon with much to learn along the way."

Understanding this truth will help us not to be too focused on the destination but enjoy the process. I've prophetic gifting and it helps me to see into the future, but the Lord has given me much grace through my wife, to help me live in the here and now.

The God of creation has given us natural seasons to teach his people about spiritual seasons. This is articulated clearly in the book of Ecclesiastes.

There is a time for everything and a season for every activity under heaven. He has made everything beautiful in its time, (Ecclesiastes 3:1,11)

Through the sixty one years of my life, I'm learning to identify and appreciate the different seasons I've been in. It's not easy to discern this with natural eyes but only by the spirit.

One of my good friends, Leo Free, taught an insightful message on needing Jesus' glasses. It's having an eternal perspective that beholds the unseen realm. "We live by faith not by sight." 2 Corinthians5:7

The Holy Spirit impressed upon Vicki and I to share the things we've learned with other sojourners, to help them in their pilgrimage.

We've taken fifteen of the many prophetic songs that the Lord has given to Vicki and I've taught on the revelatory meanings of each. I believe this book contains most of the important tenets of the Christian faith.

As you read this book, I pray that you can relate to our experiences, be encouraged and instructed, and lastly to know God is with you in everything.

CHAPTER 1

Behold a Seed

"Behold a seed and see how, see how it grows.
Life is inside of that seed and it's waiting to bring forth fruit.
Smell the air, hear the breeze, look and see the flowers.
These are the signs, the signs of springtime.
I trust you Holy Spirit, to envelope my life.
And my roots will seek your warmth in the depth of
your love.
Behold that seed and see how, see how it's grown.
Oh Lord, I wanna go on, growing up in you, I wanna
go on.
I'm a tree of righteousness, the planting of Jesus,
To bring, bring forth fruit, I wanna bring forth fruit.
Behold this seed and see how, see how it grows.
The breath of the Lord is upon those who seek his face,
and they shall be filled with their glorious inheritance.
My desire, this is my hope, that we will walk together,
filled with all your fullness, in the springtime of our lives."

(Vicki Parks)

In Genesis 1:11-12, it is written: "Then God said, let the land produce vegetation, seed bearing plants and trees on the land that bear fruit with seed in it, according to their various kinds and it was so. The land produced vegetation, plants bearing seed according to their kinds and trees bearing fruit with seed in it according to their kinds. And God saw that it was good."

In his creation, God saw the seed as the procreator of life. The seed produced the tree that brought forth the fruit.

This is the cycle of natural life, with the seed being the origin. When God looks at a seed, He sees an orchard. He sees the end from the beginning.

When God spoke that the land produce vegetation, He was establishing the principle of reproduction. Everything reproduces after its own kind.

God made man after his own image and likeness. That's why the fall was so devastating because we literally broke the mold.

Man could no longer reproduce in God's image or likeness. Death brought an end to the cycle of life.

In the first chapter of Genesis it's recorded that God said and things came into being. His words were as seeds bringing life to everything that He desired. He's the life giving spirit filling the earth.

The seed for my wife, Vicki, and I was that we were raised in good Christian homes. We both believed in Jesus Christ as children and had a good foundation for our lifes. That seed was nurtured some by our attending church and receiving basic teaching from the bible.

This incredible principle is reiterated in Genesis 8:22.

"After Noah and his family came out of the ark God told him, as long as the earth endures, seedtime and harvest, cold and heat, summer and winter, day and night will never cease."

The creative force of God can't be snuffed out like a candle. He sustains it by His mighty power. The Lord set the earth in divine order to provide for every need of mankind.

The reality of this is experienced by every person on the face of the earth. Many try to slow down or speed up this process but are unsuccessful.

Time can be your friend if you live and walk in the spirit. We need time to grow in our faith and develop in character.

In Matthew 13:18-22, Jesus explains to his disciples, what the parable of the sower meant.

"Listen then to what the parable of the sower means. When anyone hears the message about the kingdom and does not understand it, the evil one comes and snatches away what was sown in his heart. This is the seed sown along the path. The one who received the seed that fell on rocky places is the man who hears the word and at once receives it with joy. But since he has no root, he last only a short time. When trouble or persecution comes because of the word, he quickly falls away. The one who received the seed that fell among the thorns is the man who hears the word, but the worries of this life and the deceitfulness of wealth choke it, making it unfruitful. But the one who received the seed that fell on good soil is the man who hears the word and understands it. He produces a crop, yielding a hundred, sixty, or thirty times what was sown."

The seed is the life giving word of God, but it only produces fruit in good soil, which represents the heart of man. I can't stress enough, the importance of the word of God. Spiritual growth is enhanced and maintained by a steady diet of God's word. Our faith grows from hearing his word. Divine guidance and counsel come from the word of the Lord.

Like you, we have gone through different seasons of disciplining and pruning. It's important to understand that each season has its own unique purpose.

Discipline is administered to us by our loving Heavenly Father when we sin, realigning us with him. Pruning is to help us get our priorities right and deal with the self life.

We have learned to see the beauty of each season, no matter how painful it maybe. It's by abiding in Him and His word that fruit is produced. He's the source of all life. Life begins and continues in God's word.

I spend an inordinate amount of time reading and studying the bible because it's so vital to me. Many Christians say that they don't have the time to read or study their bibles. We make time for the things that are important to us.

Have you considered God's word to be this important? Has it been a priority of your life?

I've been hearing the word 'priority' in my inner man the last several years. Jesus told us not to be consumed with the things of this world but to seek first the kingdom of God.

Any good farmer knows that after you plant the seed, it needs to be nurtured. Agriculture isn't an easy business and has many facets to it. Weather can vary and bring extreme conditions of drought, hail storms, extreme wind, or flooding. Weeds need to be controlled or they will hinder the growth of the plants. Insects can destroy the crops if not maintained.

Some of these things can be controlled and others can't. It's hard to imagine anyone in this vocation that doesn't have faith. Listen to what the Lord says about this through his prophet, Isaiah.

"As the rain and the snow come down from heaven and do not return to it without watering the earth and making it bud and flourish, so that it yields seed for the sower and bread for the eater, so is my word that goes out from my mouth. It will not return to me empty, but will accomplish what I desire and achieve the purpose for which I sent it." Isaiah 55:10-11

Remember the potential of a seed and guard it with your life!

CHAPTER 2

Fill Me Up

Oh Lord I seek your love.
Oh Lord I seek your love.
Draw me Lord into your love.
Draw me Lord, draw me Lord.
Your love is sweeter than wine,
Your love is so much sweeter than wine.
It's as ointment poured forth,
Pour it forth, pour it fourth.
I'm pure through your word as a virgin,
cleansed by your blood and love.
Draw me Lord, Draw me Lord.
To savour the depth of your wine.
I thirst, my Lord, for you.
To be refreshed, my Lord, by you.
Into your chambers we'll go together.
And at your table we two will sup.
Fill me up, Lord, fill me up.
Fill me up, my prayer is fill me up.

(Vicki Parks)

Jesus said, in the famous sermon on the mount,"blessed are those who hunger and thirst for righteousness for they will be filled." Matthew 5:6

Many give lip service to a desire for more of God, yet go through life empty of his presence or blessing. I've wondered about this for many years and I believe the Lord has shown me the reasons why God's people miss it.

Let's look at the Jesus' assessment of the church in Laodicea. It shows us one of the main reasons that Christians don't enter into the fullness of a relationship with the Lord. In Revelation 3:17, it is written:

"You say I am rich, I have acquired wealth and do not need a thing. But you do not realize that you are wretched, pitiful, poor, blind and naked."

People have to see their need before they desire anything else. Sometimes, circumstances of life come and strip us of the things that we depend on. During this time, we can look to ourselves, others, or to God.

This can turn into a vicious cycle of being in need, then getting temporary relief, like the children of Israel. When things were going well they forgot about God.

"When the Lord your God brings you into the land he swore to your fathers, to Abraham, Isaac, and Jacob, to give you, a land with large, flourishing cities you did not build, houses filled with all kinds of good things you did not provide, wells you did not dig, and vineyards and olive groves you did not plant, then when you eat and are satisfied, be careful that you do not forget the Lord, who brought you out of Egypt, out of the land of slavery." Deuteronomy 6:10-12

There's something about the human nature, when it feels secure and comfortable, that it doesn't want anything else. Some, however do turn to the Lord with their whole heart, knowing only He can meet their greatest need.

After a three month separation, my wife and I saw our desperate need for God. We got connected with a small charismatic church called the Ninety First Psalm. The pastor taught us about the integrity of God's word. Later, he did a series of teaching on the Holy Spirit.

One Sunday night service, the pastor had prayer for those who wanted to receive the Holy Spirit. We were so ready and went to the front of the auditorium. Vicki and I were gloriously filled with the Holy Spirit.

There is another group of people who are filled with unbelief and don't trust in God. These are the ones who never get plugged into the local church and are church hoppers. They seem to be drawn to the latest fad and wander aimlessly, not realizing that it's a curse.

In Hebrews 11:6 it says,"And without faith it is impossible to please God because anyone who comes to Him must believe that He exist and that He rewards those who earnestly seek Him."

Trusting in God is so much more than getting our basic needs met. It's a matter of believing that He loves us and wants an intimate relationship, not allowing anything to hinder us. Let's look at what Jesus had to say about this in John 17:3.

"Now this is eternal life, that they may know you, the only true God, and Jesus Christ, whom you have sent."

This is the beginning of new life but how far we can go, no one has yet discovered. Intimacy is something that needs to be cultivated by time and commitment but the rewards are truly out of this world. This needs to be the priority of our lifes.

The accuser of the brethren tries to keep us under so much condemnation that we can't imagine God's amazing grace and His loving forgiving heart.

In Romans 2:14 it states,"Or do you show contempt for the

riches of His kindness, tolerance, and patience, not realizing that God's kindness leads you toward repentance."

Our Heavenly Father isn't beating you down when you sin or make mistakes. He is purposely redirecting your life to greener pastures.

I read a commentary on shepherd's care for their sheep. It stated that sometimes sheep would wander away from green pastures to barren land and the shepherd would have to break their legs or they would starve to death. This seems extreme but it's necessary.

James 3:2 says,"We all stumble in many ways." We need God's grace, power, and wisdom to navigate the troubled waters of life. Jesus told us that we would have trouble in this life.

The Lord has been stirring up a Godly dissatisfaction within

His people, in recent years, for anything less than an abiding

relationship with Him. Many are sick and tired of being sick and tired.

God is raising up a remnant of set apart saints who live for nothing else but Him. They seem to be moving the opposite direction of the masses as if swimming upstream.

They aren't interested in the latest Christian fads or busy religious activities. Only getting alone with Jesus will satisfy the longing in their hearts.

There were notable differences in our lifes after being baptized in the Holy Spirit. We had such a hunger for God's word that would require late nights of reading it. I carried a small new testament in my back pocket when I went to work, to read during my lunch breaks. Vicki wasn't as discreet and would take her giant sized Dake's bible to work.

Our prayer life took on a new dimension of really being in God's will. Prayer that used to be a burden became a delight. Boldness to witness and testify of God's goodness was our passion.

Do you want to join this moving of the Holy Spirit into the depths of His desire? Hebrews 12: 1 tells us,"Let us throw off everything that hinders and the sin that so easily entangles, and let us run with perseverance the race marked out for us."

We need to be single of mind and purpose. The Lord gave me the word 'resolute' several years ago. It sounded good but I really didn't know what it meant. Then I found help in the scriptures. It says,"Because the sovereign Lord helps me I will not be disgraced. Therefore have I set my face like flint, and I know I will not be put to shame."

Jesus set his face like flint to do his father's will. It's hard to stop someone who's this committed. Let's examine our own commitment and see if it measures up.

I know that it's been very convicting to look not only to my activities but to my motives. Do I have morning devotions just to punch in my time card or to spend quality time with my to Heavenly Father? Do I serve to be seen by others or out of compassion?

Lately, when I consider being filled, I've been troubled by thoughts of why and with what. During the Charismatic Renewal, many of God's people wanted to receive the Holy Spirit to have the gifts. It sounds like the biblical account of Simon the sorcerer in the eighth chapter of Acts.

Many of us who have received the precious infilling of the Holy Spirit know what a wonderful gift He is. It's been my quest to know the Father's desire.

Luke 12:32 states,"Do not be afraid, little flock, for your father has been pleased to give you the kingdom."

Sometimes, we think that we are trying to overcome God's reluctance, when it's His desire anyway.

I would like to end this chapter with a prayer for the Ephesians which speaks to what we're to be filled with.

"For this reason I kneel before the father, from whom his whole family in heaven and on earth derives its name. I pray that out of his glorious riches he may strengthen you with power through his spirit in your inner being, so that Christ may dwell in your hearts through faith. And I pray that you, being rooted and established in love, may have power together with all the saints, to grasp how wide and long and high and deep is the love of Christ, and to know this love that surpasses knowledge, that you may be filled to the measure of all of the fullness of God." Ephesians 3:14-19.

CHAPTER 3

From Grace To Face

"Oh my children you know my grace,
now my children it's time to seek my face.
For it's line upon line, from grace to face.
From faith to faith and grace to face.
My grace is sufficient for all your needs.
Now my children I'm drawing you to your knees.
It's in the Spirit we build and the flesh will yield.
Don't settle for less but seek my best.
Be bold in the Spirit, my best is yet to gain.
Build your house in prayer, don't labor in vain.
My face will be found as you kneel before my throne.
I'll not hold back from you, you're my very own.
For it's line upon line, from grace to face.
From faith to faith and grace to face.

(Vicki Parks)

Let's start this chapter with a question. How many of you have learned that the more you try, the harder it gets? Watchman Nee put it this way."The basic difficulty of a servant of God lies in the failure of the inward man to break through the outward man." (The Release of the Spirit)

The beginning of grace is to trust instead of revving up more RPMs of our own effort. The breaking of the self life isn't easy but is necessary if we are to come into the fuller measure of the Lord.

When we first came to Christ to receive salvation there was a revelation given to us from Ephesians 2:8-9."For it is by grace you have been saved, through faith and this not from yourselves, it is the gift of God, not by works, so that no one can boast."

Initially, the Christian believes the grace of God to be saved but then feels he needs something else to live the life.

Jesus last words on the cross were,"It is finished." John 19:30

That didn't mean his life was over and the Romans had done everything that they could do to him but that redemption had been fully purchased by his blood.

Self effort or obeying the law are usually the direction that people go when they don't understand this. Neither one is dependent on God and will end in futile disappointment. Paul writing to the Galatians said,"Are you so foolish? After beginning with the Spirit are you now trying to attain your goal by human effort? Galatians 3:3

So much of humanity is striving to live up to a self imposed standard of what they think God requires. It's the list of 'Dos and Don'ts' causing endless frustration and sorrow.

Many religions are birthed out of a desire to measure up to God. The difference between religion and true Christianity is ; In religion, man attempts to save himself but in Christianity, he knows only Christ can save him.

In our first couple of years of walking with Christ, Vicki and I had some adjustments to make concerning what was God's responsibility and what was ours.

I'm a small man and that probably stirred up that overachiever gene in me. I always did more than what was required. Vicki was a realist and based things on logic. This made it easy for us to perform all of the religious duties we felt obligated to.

In this atmosphere of religious activity come Jesus saying,"Come to me, all you who are weary and burdened, and I will give you rest. Take my yoke upon you and learn from me, for I am gentle and humble in heart, and you will find rest for your souls. For my yoke is easy and my burden is light." Matthew 11:28-30

This is in stark contrast to what had been going on. Jesus wasn't multitasking and filling His calendar up. He was moving with compassion to those who the Father directed Him to.

There is a simplicity to the truth and it isn't rocket science. John the Baptist had it right, when he said," more of Jesus and less of me." John 3:30

The apostle Paul stated,"You who are trying to be justified by law have been alienated from Christ. You have fallen away from grace." Galatians 5:4

This is the only scripture in the bible that mentions 'falling from grace'. It wasn't because of sin or disobedience but by trying to be justified by the law. When anyone does this, it's the same as saying that Christ' blood wasn't enough.

Anything that you add to grace isn't grace! It's like adding water to oil, it doesn't mix. Let's consider how we posture ourselves to receive this grace.

James tells us,"But He gives us more grace. That is why scripture says God opposes the proud but gives grace to the humble." James 4:6

Humility and brokenness have two sides to them. One is seeing our need and the other is seeing God's provision. That's were faith comes in, to believe in a good and faithful God.

There isn't a need that we have, that He doesn't have the provision for. It's already there before we ask but God wants us to ask and participate in the process.

In Hebrews 4:16 it says,"Let us then approach the throne of grace with confidence so that we may receive mercy and find grace to help us in our time of need."

Isn't it great to know that we have a place to go during difficult times. As amazing as grace is, there's something greater. It's his face!

Grace isn't released just to meet our basic needs but to bring us into a relationship with God himself.

When Adam and Eve were in the Garden of Eden, God would come to them in the cool of the day to have fellowship. They fell in disobedience and lost their relationship with him.

God never ceased to have a desire to fellowship with mankind and in His foreknowledge sent Jesus Christ to redeem what was lost to God and man.

If we don't believe this, we'll have a difficult time understanding the gospel. It's out of God's great love that He redeemed us to be His people, the bride of Christ.

God began stirring up a desire within us to know Him more intimately. This is when He revealed to me that meditation was more than simply reading the bible but pondering what it said. Prayer wasn't just making request but waiting on God to see what He desired.

Everything began to change from the superficial to the depths with a zeal for more. Things that we had assumed, we no longer took for granted.

Intimacy is His idea not ours. There have been some throughout the ages who have responded to His overtures of love.

Enoch so longed for God that he got so close to His heart that death couldn't claim him. When Moses left the tent of meeting, Joshua lingered in the presence of God.

David, while tending his father's sheep, sang songs of praise that filled the starry sky. Jeremiah had God's words shut up in him like fire in his bones. Jeremiah 20:9

The apostle John laid his head upon the breast of Jesus to hear his heart beat and wouldn't let Him out of his sight. The apostle Paul considered all things loss for the excellency of knowing Christ.

One of the greatest promises in the bible is James 4:8 which says,"Come near to God and He'll come near to you." Some have purposed to do this completely.

Without a doubt, one of the most awesome statements in the bible is made in Revelation 3:20."Here I am! I stand at the door and knock. If anyone hears my voice and opens the door, I will come in and eat with him and he with me."

This door is out hearts and Jesus is the one knocking. The letter is written to the church not to unbelievers. He is making the first move towards us. What will our response be? For many He waits so long.

What is the reluctance of God's people? Is it because they don't feel worthy? Let's remember what Paul wrote to the Ephesians.

"To the praise of the glory of His grace, where in He hath made us accepted in the beloved." Ephesians 1:6 KJV God has ordained us to take our place with Him.

Our Heavenly Father has called us to a life of love. If you are looking only to His hands to meet your needs, then you need to look up higher to see the tear in His eye, longing for your embrace.

It's time to go from grace to face!

CHAPTER 4

Death of Submission

"Jesus humbled himself to death,
to show a more excellent way.
It's a death we must partake of,
to walk in his excellent way.
It's a death of submission,
that releases the power of God.
As we submit to one another,
we humble ourselves to the Lord.
Humble yourself in the sight of the Lord.
There's power in submission,
for it's written in God's word.
As we humble ourselves before Him,
The Lord will lift us up in His power.
And He will lift you up, higher and higher,
and He will lift you up."

(Vicki Parks)

Jesus is our perfect example of true submission. In Phillipians 2:5-8 it says,"Your attitude should be the same as that of Christ Jesus, who being in very nature God, did not consider equality with God something to be grasped but made himself nothing, taking the very nature of a servant, being made in human likeness and being found in appearance as a man, he humbled himself and became obedient to death even death on a cross."

This was faith and obedience working in tandem. Jesus had told his disciples that this is why He had come. When He prayed in the garden of Gethsemane, Jesus broke through to resolution.

"Then Jesus went with His disciples to a place called Gethsemane, and He said to them, sit here while I go over there and pray. He took Peter and the two sons of Zebedee along with Him, and He began to be sorrowful and troubled. Then He said to them, my soul is overwhelmed with sorrow to the point of death. Stay here and keep watch with me. Going a little farther, He fell with his face to the ground and prayed, my father if it is possible, may this cup be taken from me. Yet not as I will but as you will." Matthew 26:36-39

Jesus was allowing God's will to be His own, not pursuing another course. It was painful, knowing that for the first time, He would be separated from His father because of the world's sin being placed on Him.

Jesus knew that God's calling would take him to Calvary to be crucified and shed his blood to redeem mankind.

Jesus told his disciples,"If anyone would come after me, he must deny himself and take up his cross and follow me. For whoever wants to save his life will lose it, but whoever loses his life for me will find it." Matthew 16:24-25

This was a totally new concept for me as I grew up in the sixties. The slogan for our generation was, "do your own thing." The Holy Spirit began convicting me of my independent lifestyle.

Vicki wasn't as strong willed as I was, so His dealings in her life were much gentler. When God uncovered our self life, we were amazed at the stronghold it had become and the importance of being free from it.

In our modern world the thought or act of surrendering to another isn't a popular concept. Unfortunately, this idea hasn't appealed to the church either.

Everything within our human nature screams out to be in control. The life of faith changes this dynamic by looking to God's sovereign choice.

The most basic element of faith is reliance. We need God for everything, especially for helping us to make right choices. A scripture that has really helped me with this is Psalm 37:4.

"Delight yourself in the Lord and He will give you the desires of your heart." When I first saw this scripture, I thought it sounded like a pretty good deal as it benefited me.

As I continued to meditate on it, I saw it from God's perspective. The more that we delight in the Lord, the more His desires become our desires.

This is why Jesus told His disciples that the self life had to be dealt with before they could make any progress in the kingdom of God. This is a clear call to anyone who would follow our Lord.

Abraham was dealt with in this matter as the father of our faith. In Genesis 22:1-12 it says;

"Some time later God tested Abraham. He said to him, Abraham! Here I am he replied. Then God said, take your son, your only son, Isaac, whom you love, and go to the region of Moriah. Sacrifice him there as a burnt offering on one of the mountains I will tell you about.

Early the next morning Abraham got up and saddled his donkey. He took with him two of his servants and his son Isaac. When he had cut enough wood for the burnt offering, he set out for the place God had told him about. On the third day Abraham looked up and saw the place in the distance. He said to his servants, stay here with the donkey while I and the boy go over there. We will worship and then we will come back to you. Abraham took the wood for the burnt offering and placed it on his son Isaac, and he himself carried the fire and the knife.

As the two of them went on together, Isaac spoke up and said to his father Abraham, father? Yes my son? Abraham replied. The fire and wood are here, Isaac said, but where is the lamb for the burnt offering? Abraham answered, God himself will provide the lamb for the burnt offering, my son and the two of them went on together.

When they reached the place God had told him about, Abraham built an altar there and arranged the wood on it. He bound his son Isaac and laid him on the altar, on top of the wood. Then he reached out his hand and took the knife to slay his son.

But the angel of the Lord called out to him form heaven, Abraham! Abraham! Here I am he replied. Do not lay a hand on the boy, he said. Do not do anything to him. Now I know that you fear God, because you have not withheld from me your son, your only son."

You need to remember that Isaac wasn't just a natural son but that he represented God's covenant to Abraham of being the father of many nations.

Abraham had walked with God many years before he came to this ultimate place of testing. Years earlier, he had told others that his wife Sarah was his sister to protect himself.

During a famine, Abraham went up to Egypt. He had his moments of indecisiveness when rash decisions were made. Now Abraham had given everything to God and had no rivals in his heart.

There was a time when God asked me to give my wife and children to him. I struggled with this request as they meant everything to me. He finally broke through my fears and inhibitions and revealed to me that they were safe in his care.

When I released them to him, freedom from possession brought great peace and confidence.

This is where every true child of God must come. We possess nothing and He is our all in all. Whatever you require of me, Heavenly Father, I will give you.

My life isn't my own but has been purchased by Christ blood! As He has given all, I can do no less. Lead me in this life of submission to die to everything that is not of you.

CHAPTER 5

Fellowship His Sufferings

I've reached a crossroad in my life,
That can end all my strife.
I hear His voice say to me,
are you able to drink my cup?
A decision must be made today.
Do I really want to know Him?
Am I able to endure today,
the cross standing in my way?
I'll fellowship his sufferings,
that conform me to His death.
For the prize I see set before me,
is that I'm to be the bride of Christ.
As a horse in Pharoah's chariot,
I am swift in His pursuit.
I'll not grieve or quench this ardent zeal,
I am ready for what is real.

(Vicki Parks)

After a very fruitful ministry and at the end of his life, Paul wanted one thing only. To know Christ in everyway possible but seemingly not in all ways desirable. In Phillipians 3:10 it says;

"I want to know Christ and the power of his resurrection and the fellowship of sharing in his sufferings, becoming like him in his death, and so, somehow, to attain to the resurrection from the dead."

Most of us would like the power that Christ exhibited while He walked on earth but not the suffering and death. In the last chapter I wrote about the death of submission, that parallels this chapter.

Many years ago, Vicki and I entered a new season of experiencing our physical weaknesses. During the Christmas holidays, Vicki was showering and felt a lump on her breast. She told me about it and I encouraged her to get some test to see what it was.

The doctor did a cat scan and then a biopsy. The test was positive that she had cancer. This was a shock to both of us as we had been healthy all of our lifes.

I called the elders and asked them to come to our house and pray for Vicki. As they prayed for her, God gave me a prophetic word that "this sickness wasn't unto death but for the glory of God."

Vicki invited the Lord in, during this difficult trial. Her breast surgeon recommended chemo therapy, a mastectomy, and reconstructive surgery.

Vicki went through the chemo sessions every three weeks for about three months. She was such a trooper and never complained. She didn't miss a day of work, even though her boss told her to take off all of the time that she needed.

During this time, I was her caregiver, prepared the meals, and kept the house clean. It was such a blessing to serve in such a tangible way.

All of her co-workers, clients, family, and brethren were amazed by her upbeat attitude and faith she displayed during this extreme situation.

It's a new paradigm from the survival mode that many live in. Several years ago, God told me that He was opening my eye to His eternal perspective. Things have never been the same since that time.

Our Lord sees the big picture, the end from the beginning. The writer of Hebrews put it this way. "Let us fix our eyes on Jesus, the author and perfector of our faith, who for the joy set before him endured the cross, scorning its shame, and sat down at the right hand of the throne of God." Hebrews 12:2

Jesus knew there was an eternal reward for His temporal sacrifice. That was the joy He had to make it.

In 2 Corinthians 4:17-18 it's written, "For our light and momentary troubles are achieving for us an eternal glory that far outweighs them all. So we fix our eyes not on what is seen but on what is unseen. For what is seen is temporary but what is unseen is eternal.

Paul was truly tapping into the mind of Christ when he wrote this. It enabled him to follow Christ wherever He went. There is a saying that many people are too heavenly minded to be any earthly good but I think the reverse is true. Many people are too earthly minded to be any heavenly good.

There was a certain account told to me by an African missionary. He and some nationals were traveling in the back of a pick up truck to a remote village. It began raining abundantly and all of the men in the back of the truck started to complain. In the field, they were passing by, was a farmer raising his hands to praise God for a much needed rain on his drought stricken field.

Unfortunately, most of us see things through the filter of how things effect us personally to whether it's good or not. In the kingdom of God there's always a price to pay and the benefit is usually for others.

In 1Peter 2:20-21 it says, "But how is it to your credit if you receive a beating for doing wrong and endure it? But if you suffer for doing good and you endure it, this is commendable before God. To this you were called, because Christ suffered for you, leaving you an example that you should follow in his steps."

Jesus example was one of self sacrifice and loving the outcast of society. He cared nothing for a reputation and acceptance of man. Wandering like a nomad, He didn't enjoy the comforts of a home.

When my family and I went on the mission field to southern Mexico, God gave us a word to travel light. We received this not only in the natural scheme of things but also spiritually. It's amazing how well you can advance without all of the weight of insignificance.

Peter tells us, "Dear friends, do not be surprised at the painful trial you are suffering, as though something strange were happening to you. But rejoice that you participate in the sufferings of Christ, so that you may be overjoyed when his glory is revealed. If you are insulted because of the name of Christ, you are blessed, for the spirit of glory and of God rest on you. If you suffer it should not be as a murderer or thief or any other kind of criminal, or even as a meddler. However, if you suffer as a Christian, do not be ashamed, but praise God that you bear that name. For it is time for judgement to begin with the family of God, and if it begins with us, what will the outcome be for those who do not obey the gospel of God? And if it is hard for the righteous to be saved, what will become of the ungodly and the sinner? So then those who suffer according to God's will should commit themselves to their faithful creator and continue to do good." 1 Peter 4:12-19

Committing ourselves to God is the substructure of a life of faith. When the elders came to pray for Vicki, they asked me how I was doing. I told them that I had never been down this road before and didn't know how far that it would go but I knew God was with us.

When Vicki invited the Lord into the trial of having cancer, she was fellowshipping his sufferings. It was the best thing that she could have done. That's why she wasn't stressed out, fearful, or full of unbelief.

The portion of scripture written earlier from 1 Peter 4:12-19, really sums up what I've been trying to say. It's all for the glory of God and He will keep us in His loving grace.

CHAPTER 6

The Mary and Martha Gap

Your body is so weak my Lord,
There's a gap in your body.
Who can heal your body Lord,
of this Mary and Martha gap?
The spiritual Mary's on one side,
at your feet, looking into your face.
The serving Martha's on the other side,
seeing needs and serving with grace.
There's a gap in between them Lord,
and to you this is not pleasing.
This gap that's in your body Lord,
stops the flow of your word.
The body of Christ is an army,
rising to stand and fight.
The head would say it's much better,
to fight with all of your might.
There need not be any gap my Lord,
your ways are higher, they're much higher than that.
Bring us together, bring us together Lord,
hand in hand we'll stand in the gap.

(Vicki Parks)

There is an incident recorded in Luke 10:38-42 where two sisters had a different approach to Jesus.

"As Jesus and his disciples were on their way, He came to a village where a woman named Martha opened her home to Him. She had a sister called Mary, who sat at the Lord's feet listening to what He said.

But Martha was distracted by all the preparations that had to be made. She came to Him and asked, Lord, don't you care that my sister has left me to do the work by myself?

Tell her to help me! Martha, Martha, the Lord answered, you are worried and upset about many things, but only one thing is needed. Mary has chosen what is better and it will not be taken away from her."

There are many things in this particular passage worthy of discussion but there is one that almost jumps off the page. Martha was distracted! From what and by what? She was distracted from Jesus, by serving Him.

Many of us, that have been in full time ministry for awhile, can identify with Martha and her dilemma.

Right out of bible school, I began working with a small church in the west Texas area as an associate pastor. Vicki became the church's secretary.

There were some good devout people in the congregation but it became apparent to us that no one was serving in any capacity. We talked with the pastor and elders about starting helps ministries to strengthen the church.

They were in agreement that there was a need for it but didn't know what to do. I told them that I would take the leadership role and train all of those that would volunteer.

I presented this idea to the church and many committed to participate in serving. It was a wonderful experience to see different ones discover their gifts and how to use them to minister to the body.

There was great excitement and enthusiasm during this time but some were stirred to increase their devotional time with the Lord and intercession.

Unfortunately, with every move of God, the enemy works to bring division. Before long, those who were actively involved in serving were complaining about those who weren't. This caused others to think that those in helps ministries didn't see the value of the spiritual disciplines.

All of us leaders, seeing what was happening, brought the church together for a meeting of repentance. It really cleared the air and brought much needed unity amongst us.

Through this experience and revelation from the word of God, we began to see an unnecessary Mary and Martha gap. Also, what the church can do to close this gap to bring us together.

"Hearing that Jesus had silenced the Sadducees, the Pharisees got together. One of them, an expert in the law, tested Him with this question: Teacher, which is the greatest commandment in the law? Jesus replied: Love the Lord your God with all you heart and with all your soul and with all your mind. This is the first and greatest commandment." Matthew 22: 34-38

How many of us have served the work of the Lord instead of the Lord or the work? He has to be the priority of our lifes. His kingdom is built relationally. Our motivation to serve should be to obey and honor Him.

What happened to Martha, was that she was so caught up in serving Jesus that she didn't have time to listen to what He was saying. This can happen to us as well. The momentum of doing good works can carry us past divine appointments with our Lord.

When my family and I were on the mission field in Mexico, I had a very sobering spiritual dream. I was on a very large roller coaster and was wanting to get off. When I looked down, there to wasn't anyone at the controls. The Holy Spirit said, "if you want to get off, then you'll have to jump."

I said, "I rebuke you devil", but I knew it was the Lord. I had gotten caught up in doing typical ministry stuff and God had other plans. When I woke up, I told the Lord that I would do whatever He wanted me to do.

He replied, that I come to Mexico to do a work for Him but I was the work that He was doing.

The other part of this encounter with Mary and Martha is the concept for the equality of the work. Martha is wanting Jesus to get Mary to help her.

There is an underlying perspective of comparison her between the two sisters. It's another thing keeping Martha from Jesus.

"We do not dare to classify or compare ourselves with some who commend themselves. When they measure themselves by themselves and compare themselves with themselves, they are not wise." 2 Corinthians 10:12

Paul knew what he was talking about as people were always criticizing him. You never win with comparisons as someone is always better than you and someone isn't as good. You're never the king of the hill.

"Jesus called them together and said, you know that those who are regarded as rulers of the gentiles lord it over them, and their high officials exercise authority over them. Not so with you. Instead, who ever wants to become great among you must be your servant, and whoever wants to be first must be slave of all. For even the Son of Man did not come to be served but to serve and to give His life as a ransom for many." Mark 10:42-45

Jesus is our example and in the scripture just stated, it says that He came to serve. Sometimes, there is a tendency to have a certain perspective about what is spiritual and what isn't.

Only God knows our motives. Why we do the things that we do. Let's look at what Jesus had to say about this.

"The one who sent me is with me, He has not left me alone, for I always do what pleases Him." John 8:29

This puts service in a different light of who we do it for, instead of going through the motions of just doing it.

"So whether you eat or drink or whatever you do, do it all for the glory of God." 1 Corinthians 10:31

When our priorities are divinely aligned, then are motives will be pure and our service will be freighted with God's enabling grace.

There need not be any gap or division in the church when we understand that we are interdependent and one in the fulfillment of God's eternal purpose.

CHAPTER 7

His Faithfulness will not Fail

"The Lord bestows strength on His warriors
and with His holy oil He anoints them.
His arm shall be their strength,
And He will crush their foes before them.
His faithfulness will not fail.
His covenant will not break.
His faithfulness will not fail.
For He has sworn by His holiness.
His faithfulness and mercy are upon us
and in His name our strength is exalted.
He is our Father, our God, and our salvation.
Thus we are higher than the kings of the earth.
Our seed will endure forever
and if transgression is in their heart,
He will visit them with His rod,
for His faithfulness will never fail.

(Vicki Parks)

When Abraham was old, he sent his chief servant to get a wife for Isaac from among his relatives in his own country. His servant traveled to the land of his forefathers and prayed that God would grant him success. He also, prayed a very specific prayer for confirmation.

"Then he prayed O Lord, God of my master Abraham, give me success today, and show kindness to my master Abraham. See, I am standing beside this spring, and the daughters of the towns people are coming out to draw water. May it be that when I say to a girl, please let down your jar that I may have a drink and she says, drink, and I'll water your camels too- let her be the one you have chosen for your servant Isaac." Genesis 24:12-14

After his prayer, God answered in a very complete way.

"Before he had finished praying Rebekah came out with her jar on her shoulder, she was the daughter of Bethuel, son of Milcah, who was the wife of Abraham's brother Nahor. The girl was very beautiful, a virgin, no man had ever lain with her. She went down to the spring, filled her jar and came up again. The servant hurried to meet her and said, please give me a little water from your jar. Drink, my lord, she said, and quickly lowered the jar to her hands and gave him a drink. After she had given him a drink, she said, I'll draw water for your camels too, until they have finished drinking." Genesis 24:15-19

"Then the man bowed down and worshiped the Lord, saying, praise be to the Lord, the God of my master Abraham, who has not abandoned his kindness and faithfulness to my master. As for me, the Lord has led me on the journey to the house of my master's relatives." Genesis 24:26-27

From the time when Abraham first heard God's voice telling him to leave his country, his people, and his father's household, he had learned to trust his word.

I still remember when the Lord revealed his calling to me. Three different scriptures kept coming to my mind. This didn't just happen for a moment but all day long.

Proverbs 3:5-6, "Trust in the Lord with all your heart and lean not on your own understanding. In all your ways acknowledge him and He will make your paths straight."

Isaiah 1:19, "If you are willing and obedient you will eat the best from the land."

Mark 16:15 "He said to them, go into all the world and preach the good news to all creation."

I really didn't know what to do with all of this, so I talked with my pastor, Cal Lorts, who confirmed the call. Vicki and I talked about it with much prayer.

We felt that I needed to go to bible school in preparation for the ministry. After checking on several different schools, there was a strong pull to Overcoming Bible Training Center in Fort Worth, Texas. It was a school founded by Jerry Savelle.

Vicki and I decided to go check it out in June, when our daughter, Sky, was out of school.

When we got to the church, where the school was, a prominent speaker was teaching. All at once the inside of the church changed and there were desks everywhere and students writing. The Holy Spirit told me that I would be there in August to attend school. He told me to go back home and sell our house and put things in order to move to Fort Worth.

I had barely digested this when the thought came to my mind, had he told my wife? Now, I thought this must have been what Abraham experienced when God told him to leave. Vicki wasn't too shook up when I told her what the Lord had said as she knew a change was coming.

When we returned back to Arizona, I told my pastor what I encountered. He was supportive but realistic concerning the transition and possible difficulties.

God had imparted to me a gift of faith and I don't think I could have doubted, even if I wanted to. Things came together really well and we were packed in our little Ford Pinto and U-Haul trailer, three small kids and all.

The last night, before we left, we spent the night with a new couple to our church. We had communion together and some awesome fellowship.

The family loaded up in the car, the next morning for our trip, when I noticed a big white envelope on the dash. There was a little note and three one hundred dollar bills. The note said, we believe God's in this and we want to be a part of it. What a great way to start the trip. Thanks, Lord!

Our family pulled into Fort Worth Wednesday afternoon and went to a Motel Six. I thought that it would be good to attend the midweek service.

It was a nice surprise that Jerry Savelle was in town and would be teaching. There was a good praise and worship before Jerry taught an anointed message on 'ministering to the necessity of the saints. The Holy Spirit moved mightily confirming His word.

Two ladies, standing close to us, asked if we had a place to stay and we told them, only at the Motel Six. They said that they had a two bedroom apartment but we could have one of the bedrooms. Then a young man came up to me and gave me a hundred dollars. What a night!

Within a couple of weeks, I found out about a house for rent by a church. I went and talked to the church staff about renting the house. They said that it was a big three bedroom house but needed repairs as their printer had lived there.

I told them, that I was pretty handy and could do the repairs. They said that my family could live there rent free as long as I did repairs on the house.

Some time later, the Lord spoke to me, during my prayer time, about a pastor in Big Spring that had a certain vision for his church and where I fit in. He told me to go see him and tell him this.

A week later, I went to see him and he told me that this was the Lord and I became his associate pastor.

I hope you didn't mind my sharing this personal testimony with you but it illustrates again, God's faithfulness. No matter what you're doing or where you're at, God is there!

Jeremiah was called the weeping prophet because he mourned Jerusalem's destruction. He wrote an account of it in the book of Lamentations describing his pain and resolution.

"I remember my affliction and my wandering, the bitterness an the gall. I well remember them, and my soul is downcast within me. Yet this I call to mind and therefore I have hope. Because of the Lord's great love we are not consumed, for His compassions never fail.

They are new every morning, great is your faithfulness. I say to myself, the Lord is my portion, therefore I will wait for him. The Lord is good to those whose hope is in Him, to the one who seeks Him, it is good to wait quietly for the salvation of the Lord." Lamentations 3:19-26

Everyone of us needs to be honest with our feelings but not dominated by them. Jesus warned us that we would have troubles in this world. John 16:33

In the passage of scripture from Lamentations that you just read, Jeremiah used two verses to describe how he felt and then six verses to show where his focus was.

You can't walk through life looking at your feet. We need to look up to the hills where our help comes from. Psalm 121:1-2

Many of us have went through enough difficulties in our lifes that we have a track record with God. Remember His past deliverances and provision during those times.

In Revelation 12:11 it says," They overcame him by the blood of the lamb and by the word of their testimony." What will your testimony be? That God is faithful and His compassions never fail or that your faith has been shipwrecked?

I pray that the Lord is your portion!

CHAPTER 8

Quietness and Confidence

"Like a weary sojourner my youthful zeal it wanes,
away from your presence, Lord, an emptiness grows
within.
A gentle voice is calling me. He says don't go your own
way,
there is rest and refreshing and quietness to be revealed.
Oh Lord I hear you call, to give you my all in quietness,
but what's to be found, Lord, as I stumble around in
quietness.
You say we have strength in quietness and confidence,
and the effect of righteousness is quietness.
My words to you, they should be few,
for a fool is known by the multitude of his words.
Where's the quietness.
Forgive my faithless wandering and make known your
path to me,
in quietness and confidence, a signpost forever to be.
I trust you Lord, for your ways are right.
I know your voice is calling me to your quiet,
I hear your quietness.

(Rob & Vicki Parks)

"The fruit of righteousness will be peace, the effect of righteousness will be quietness and confidence forever." Isaiah 32:17.

I still remember the day that I stumbled over this scripture. It sounded good but I'll admit that I didn't understand it.

A good friend of mine and spiritual father, Charlie Richards, always says that God gives us the natural to learn the spiritual. In this instance, He did just that.

At this particular time, the Lord was giving Vicki many prophetic songs, that she was releasing to the church along with her exhortations.

Something happened to her voice and she got real bad laryngitis. She went to the doctor and he told her that she had damaged her vocal chords and would need to remain silent for a month.

This was a shock to both of us but we knew the doctor was right and Vicki's health was the most important thing.

It would be hard to say who this was the most trying for, Vicki or me. I missed hearing her cheerful voice and her beautiful songs. She missed not being able to communicate with me and others.

After several weeks of this, the Holy Spirit began to show Vicki the importance of listening. It's not easy for people with vocal giftings to be quiet.

This journey started in the shallow considerations of basic truths and moved into the depths of profound revelation.

It became obvious to me, by Vicki's demeanor and lack of physical activity, that something was happening deep within her. There was a domino effect upon me and I began to desire the quietness within my soul.

An amazing transformation began happening in both of our lifes. With our mouths closed, our ears began to open wide and hear things that we had been missing.

Waiting on the Lord has become a lost art to the modern church. Much of our prayer life is a monologue with God being the silent audience.

Toward the end of Vicki's non-speaking sabbatical, the Holy Spirit gave us the song, that is at the beginning of this chapter. It's the only one that we've written together.

I would like to end this chapter with opening up the scripture that we started with from Isaiah 32:17.

It's righteousness that releases peace, quietness, and confidence. Where do we get this righteousness?

"Therefore, if anyone is in Christ, he is a new creation. The old has gone, the new has come. All this is from God who reconciled us to himself through Christ and gave us the ministry of reconciliation, that God was reconciling the world to himself in Christ, not counting men's sins against them. And He has committed to us the message of reconciliation. We are therefore Christ ambassadors as though God were making his appeal through us. We implore you on Christ behalf, be reconciled to God. God made him who had no sin to be sin for us, so that in him we might become the righteousness of God." 2 Corinthians 5:17-21.

I felt that it was important to write this complete scripture text for you to see God's fuller purpose in what Christ did for us in this great exchange.

Our sin for his righteousness. That is God's gift to us. The perfect righteousness of Christ. Our debt has been paid for and we are now in right standing with God.

If this doesn't give you peace, than nothing else will. The accuser of the brethren can come to you and tell you that you've failed and aren't righteous. Agree with him and tell him that you have Christ righteousness and that it's more than enough.

Know that, peace isn't an emotion of the flesh but a fruit of the Spirit. When we're living in the reality of the kingdom of God within us, it's righteousness, peace, and joy in the Holy Spirit.

Quietness isn't just the absence of noise but the settledness of our being. Psalm 46:10 says, "Be still and know that I am God."

Much of the religious activity of this time is a clear indication that there is need for the church to have a more intimate relationship with the Lord.

Confidence can best be described by the scriptures themselves from 2 Timothy 1:12

"I know whom I have believed and am convinced that he is able to guard what I have entrusted to him for that day."

When we know the integrity, faithfulness, goodness, mercy, and power of our God, then we can trust Him.

As Paul wrote in Philippians chapter Three, "We put no confidence in the flesh." He had quite a resume but learned how futile his own efforts were.

Faith in Christ' righteousness brings us into this confidence to live an overcoming life of victory.

It's very difficult for the devil to have inroads with believers who are walking this way.

I gave a prophetic word to a very special friend of mine, Judy Yanke, some years ago. The gist of it was, "Still waters run deep".

This person is quiet and compassionate.

I'm not meaning to be critical when I say this but much of the church has been like a babbling brook, lots of noise and very shallow. We've been busy with religious activities like Martha and not attentive to Jesus' words like Mary.

This reminds me of an account of one of the greatest prophets who needed to learn this lesson of how to recognize the presence and voice of God.

"The Lord said, go out and stand on the mountain in the presence of the Lord, for the Lord is about to pass by. Then a great and powerful wind tore the mountains apart and shattered the rocks before the Lord, but the Lord was not in the wind.

After the wind there was an earthquake, but the Lord was not in the earthquake. After the earthquake came a fire, but the Lord was not in the fire. And after the fire came a gentle whisper. When Elijah heard it, he pulled his cloak over his face and went out and stood at the mouth of the cave." 1Kings 19:11-13

After almost fourty years of walking with God, I've found that He usually communicates with me in three specific ways. One of the main ways is through His written word. Another is by the Holy Spirit speaking directly to my spirit and lastly when other Christians confirm His will to me. I'm not leaving out visions or dreams but these are usually the exception and not the rule.

"Because those who are lead by the Spirit of God are sons of God." Romans 8:14 The sons in this verse comes from the Greek word 'huios', which speaks of full maturity.

When we come to this place in God, we have quietness and confidence knowing that He is in control of everything.

CHAPTER 9

Arise In My Life

"Arise in my life, arise Lord God,
arise in my life today.
Arise in life, arise Lord God,
Arise with your mighty fire.
A fire burning bright as a light dear Lord,
a light that leads the way.
To your presence Lord for all who seek,
to walk in your holy way.
Oh burn away the chaff dear Lord,
the chaff that stands in our way.
Purify our vessels Lord,
to show someone else the way.
From your throne, oh Lord, comes a flaming fire,
a fire that purifies.
How we long to live in your presence Lord,
consumed in your holy fire."

(Vicki Parks)

There is a prophetic word that speaks to what we have and who we are as born again spirit filled believers in Christ.

"Arise, shine, for your light has come, and the glory of the Lord rises upon you. See, darkness covers the earth and thick darkness is over the peoples, but the Lord rises upon you. Nations will come to your light, and kings to the brightness of your dawn." Isaiah 60:1-3

We need to better understand the new creation that each of us has become in Christ. Filled with His life, spirit, love, and power.

Jesus said that, "You are the light of the world." Matthew 5:14 The church is to reflect His light and represent Him in the earth.

When my family and I were living in Arizona, I had a vision of me going into a prison with my bible. I talked with my pastor about this and he suggested that I contact Brother Alfred who was actively doing prison ministry.

I called him and he invited me to go with him on Saturdays to a nearby prison.

He told me that the guards would bring as many prisoners that wanted to come to a holding cell, where we could minister to them. Brother Alfred told me that he would teach the word and if I felt the unction of the Spirit, then I could speak.

We learned to flow together in the Spirit and became good tag team preachers. I still remember one particular Saturday, when about thirty five prisoners came to our meeting. Brother Alfred and I felt a powerful anointing to preach and gave an invitation for them to receive Jesus.

Every prisoner, except one, came to the front of the holding area and received Christ. As we were leaving the prison, I told Brother Alfred that I had never experienced anything like that in my life. He said, "That where it's the darkest, the light shines the brightest."

"For God said, let light shine out of darkness, made his light shine in our hearts to give us the light of the knowledge of the glory of God in the face of Christ. But we have this treasure in jars of clay to show that this all surpassing power is from God and not from us." 2 Corinthians 4:6-7

Many of us are so conscious of our natural characteristics that we forget what God has deposited in us. What is the treasure that is in our earthen vessels? It's Jesus Christ by his Holy Spirit.

"Examine yourselves to see whether you are in the faith. Test yourselves. Do you not realize that Christ Jesus is in you, unless, of course you fail the test." 2 Corinthians 13:5

The reality of Christ living in us brings a new and different dynamic to our lives. When you look at the metamorphosis of a caterpillar becoming a butterfly, you get some indication of what happened to us.

Unfortunately, many of God's people still see themselves as earthbound worms and not as butterflies soaring in the sky. Our identity is really important to how we live in this world.

"For as he thinketh in his heart so is he." Proverbs 23:7 KJV This scripture basically says that the way we see ourselves, is the way we will live.

I read a story of a man who lived in Europe, back in the early twentieth century. His heart was set on going to America. He saved up all of the money that he could, to buy a ticket for a ship voyage there.

The time had come for his trip overseas and he was so excited, even though he had no money left. The ship was magnificent and the ocean beautiful. During the meal times, the man would hide for fear and embarrassment.

After several days, one of the crew members asked him why he never came to meal times. Reluctantly, he told him that he didn't have any money for the meals. The crew member told him that the meals came with the price of the ticket.

How many of us are just along for the ride and aren't partaking of all the benefits that are included.

"One day Peter and John were going up to the temple at the time of prayer at three in the afternoon. Now a man cripple from birth, was being carried to the temple gate called beautiful, where he was put everyday to beg from those going into the temple courts. When he saw Peter and John about to enter, he asked them for money. Peter looked straight at him, as did John. Then Peter said, look at us! So the man gave them his attention, expecting to get something from them. Then Peter said, silver or gold I do not have, but what I have I give you. In the name of Jesus Christ of Nazareth, walk. Taking him by the right hand, he helped him up, and instantly the man's feet and ankles became strong." Acts 3:1-7

I want you to take notice of what Peter said to the crippled man. I don't have money but what I have, I give you.

Throughout much of the latter church age, we've had lots of money but very little power. You can't give what you don't have. This needs to change!

There's been a lot of in-Christ teaching, the past thirty years. It might be time for some Christ-in us teaching. The focus has been on us and not the Lord. This is why we run into so many limitations in our Christian lifes. One scripture that has really helped me to remain balanced is Galatians 2:20

"I have been crucified with Christ and I no longer live, but Christ lives in me. The life I live in the body, I live by faith in the son of God who loved me and gave himself for me."

When we look to Christ and draw from His resources, then our witness to the world is that of overcomers.

One day, many years ago, the Holy Spirit told me that He was limitless and wanted to be limitless in me. I'll admit that this was really hard for me to wrap my mind around. It stretched me.

One morning, I was reading the gospel of John and came to an unbelievable passage of scripture in John 14:12.

"I tell you the truth, anyone who has faith in me will do what I have been doing. He will do even greater things than these because I am going to the father."

Just to believe that I could do what Jesus did is a stretch but to believe I could do greater things is off the charts.

Prayer and re-reading the scriptures that I'd been meditating on brought me to the place of realizing that there was no way I can do the extraordinary.

I needed God's grace and power, which are available in Christ. I prayed, "Arise in my life, Lord."

CHAPTER 10

Song of Deliverance

"The song of deliverance is a song of the Father's love.
It's a song that I sing, for He's shown His love to me.
A Father, for his child, will always want the best,
so there's no need to fear when it's a Father's love at test.
I'll sing at the Red Sea.
I'll sing in the face of the enemy.
My father opens blind eyes and he causes the deaf to
hear.
Yet all of this is not enough to take away my fears.
It's as I recall that He's never let me down,
and as my Father, I know, He'll always be around.
I'll sing at the Red Sea.
I'll sing in the face of the enemy.
I'll sing of His faithfulness to me.
I'll sing, my Father loves me.
As we sing this song on the right side of the sea,
the Father's love will swallow the enemy.
When He and I, together, hand in hand,
we'll walk on water.
For us there's no dry land."

(Vicki Parks)

One of the greatest deliverances ever recorded was for the Israelites at the Red Sea. Let's look at what Moses told them at the onset of this experience.

"As Pharaoh approached, the Israelites looked up, and there were the Egyptians, marching after them. They were terrified and cried out to the Lord. They said to Moses, was it because there were no graves in Egypt that you brought us to the desert to die? What have you done to us by bringing us out of Egypt? Didn't we say to you in Egypt, leave us alone, let us serve the Egyptians? It would have been better for us to serve the Egyptians than to die in the desert! Moses answered the people, do not be afraid. Stand firm and you will see the deliverance the Lord will bring you today. The Egyptians you see today you will never see again. The Lord will fight for you, you need only to be still." Exodus 14:10-14

Listen to the complaints, unbelief, and fear coming from the lips of the Israelites. Then God worked through His ordained leader to perform one of the greatest miracles ever. Boy, did their tune change! One moment murmuring and the next, one of the greatest praise songs ever recorded.

"I will sing to the Lord, for he is highly exalted. The horse and its rider he has hurled into the sea. The Lord is my strength and my song, he has become my salvation.

He is my God, and I will praise him, my father's God and I will exalt him." Exodus 15:1-2

That's just a taste of the first two verses of this eighteen verse song. It's quite descriptive and jubilant.

I read a very good and insightful teaching by the late David Wilkerson entitled "Right song on the wrong side." In this teaching, he clearly illustrates how the children of Israel should have had faith to praise and honor God before they received help.

Looking back, I remember when the Lord provided finances for a pressing need that I had. When I first received it, many exclamations of thanks came fourth. The Holy Spirit spoke clearly to my heart, that I wasn't praising Him but just relieved from the pressure of the situation.

David, who grew up tending his father's sheep, spent many hours playing his harp and singing songs of praise and worship to God. I believe those intimate times with the Lord prepared him to protect the sheep from the lion and bear. Also he was ready to lead Israel's army against their enemies.

David wrote this Psalm in remembrance of God's faithfulness in battle.

"You are my hiding place. You will protect me from trouble and surround me with songs of deliverance." Psalm 32:7

Over twenty years ago, Vicki was a worship leader and writing many prophetic songs. There was a situation with our church's leadership that was very hurtful for her.

After this, she drew back from the Lord and the church for several years. Sometime later, she was diagnosed with breast cancer. The Holy Spirit gave me a word for her from Zephaniah 3:17.

"The Lord your God is with you, He is mighty to save. He will take great delight in you, He will quiet you with His love, He will rejoice over you with singing."

During this time, Vicki was getting test before receiving chemo therapy. She was to pass through a MRI tunnel, where they usually give you sedatives but Vicki put on a head set and asked the assistant to play KLOVE on the Christian radio station.

As she was going into the tunnel, the song, "Healing Hands of God" by Jeremy Camp came on. When she left and was driving home, the song, "Healing Rain" by Michael W. Smith came on the radio. That's really being surrounded by songs of deliverance.

Vicki went through several years of chemo therapy, radiation, and surgeries but now she is healthy again. God, also, brought her inner healing and a new song.

"From the lips of children and infants you have ordained praise, because of your enemies, to silence the foe and the avenger." Psalm 8:2

This is written by David, who knew the importance and power of praise. His life was filled with songs to the Lord.

I see two sides to this Psalm. One is to direct us to God as our complete source of strength, wisdom, and ultimately victory in every circumstance of life.

The other is to know that it's powerful in spiritual warfare. Praise takes us first vertically then horizontally. One of the greatest examples of this in the bible is the account of Jehoshaphat.

"All the men of Judah, with their wives and children and little ones, stood there before the Lord. Then the Spirit of the Lord came upon Jahaziel son of Zechariah, the son of Benaiah, the son of Jeiel, the son of Mattaniah, a levite and descendant of Asaph, as he stood in the assembly. He said, listen, King Jehoshaphat and all who live in Judah and Jerusalem! This is what the Lord says to you. Do not be afraid or discouraged because of this vast army. For the battle is not yours, but God's. Tomorrow march down against them. They will be climbing up by the pass of Ziz, and you will find them at the end of the gorge in the desert of Jeruel. You will not have to fight this battle. Take up your positions, stand firm and see the deliverance the Lord will give you, O Judah and Jerusalem. Do not be afraid, do not be discouraged. Go out to face them tomorrow and the Lord will be with you. Jehoshaphat bowed with his face to the ground, and all the people of Judah and Jerusalem fell down in worship before the Lord. Then some Levites from the Kohathites and Korahites stood up and praised the Lord, the God of Israel, with a very loud voice. Early in the morning they left for the dessert of Tekoa. As they set out, Jehoshaphat stood and said, listen to me, Judah and people of Jerusalem! Have faith in the Lord your God and you will be upheld, have faith in his prophets and you will be successful. After consulting the people, Jehoshaphat appointed men to sing to the Lord and to praise him for the splendor of his holiness as they went out at the head of the army, saying, give thanks to the Lord, for his love endures forever. As they began to sing and praise, the Lord set ambushes against the men of Ammon and Moab and Mount Seir who were invading Judah, and they were defeated." 2 Chronicles 20:13-22

This is one of the greatest events in all of history where the people of God, following their faithful king, place their complete trust in God during and extreme trial.

Then, the Lord raised up a prophet to tell them that the battle was the Lord's. Jehoshaphat positioned the singers to be at the head of the army.

Our praise, should always be at the front of any spiritual warfare as God has given us a song of deliverance!

CHAPTER 11

Taste the Fear of the Lord

"Oh taste and see the Lord is good,
Blessed is the man that trust in Him.
The young lions do lack and suffer hunger,
but to them that seek the Lord, He withholds no good
thing.
Of fear the Lord, you his saints,
for there is no want to them that fear him.
Come my child, and hearken unto me,
for I would teach you, the fear of God.
It's to keep your tongue from evil and your lips from
guile.
Depart from evil, do good, seek peace,
and seek the Lord with all your heart.
Oh taste and see the fear of the Lord is good,
it's clean and it's pure, enduring forever.
Oh taste with me, the Lord, he is good,
he's sweeter than honey and the honeycomb."

(Vicki Parks)

The fear of the Lord is so much different then many of God's people have considered it to be. Some view it as dread and judgement handed down from heaven.

We imagine God to be a grouchy old man with a big stick, ready to hit us when we make mistakes. Scripture says that God loves us but we really don't think that He likes us.

It's important to have a proper perspective of the fear of the Lord or it will hinder our relationship with him. I will use the scriptures themselves to properly define what it is exactly.

"The fear of the Lord is pure." Psalm 19:9 It's unmixed and blameless. That's what Jesus purchased with His own blood. We have His righteousness to steward with a holy fear.

Compromise can't be tolerated if one is to live this way. It's all or nothing with the Lord. Coming out of the world is only part of devotion. The other part is being given to God for His purposes.

"Come my children, listen to me, I will teach you the fear of the Lord. Whoever of you loves life and desires to see many good days, keep your tongue from evil and your lips from speaking lies. Turn from evil and do good, seek peace and pursue it." Psalm 34:11-14.

Isn't it amazing that the first thing addressed is the tongue. The book of James has a clear description of what destruction it can bring.

If you fear the Lord, your words will be few and well chosen. That's why God ordained praise to be in our mouths.

It's vitally important for us to understand what God loves and what He hates. The Lord loves righteousness and hates evil.

He has watched mankind, since the fall, destroy each other. Violence, filth, and corruption have covered the landscape and polluted our society.

I don't believe man realizes how far that we've fallen. Our society has embraced relativity and abandoned all that is absolute.

The mantra of our day is, "If it feels good, do it." This fits a carnal fleshly lifestyle really well but sidesteps the cross of Christ.

To come into agreement with God, Proverbs 8:13 says, "To fear the Lord is to hate evil. I hate pride and arrogance, evil behavior and perverse speech."

When we begin to see evil for what it is and how destructive it can be, also dishonoring to our God, then we should want no part of it.

Let's look at some positive aspects of the fear of the Lord, as there are many.

"The fear of the Lord is the beginning of wisdom. All who follow his precepts have good understanding. To him belongs eternal praise." Psalm 111:10

How many of us need the wisdom of God to handle the affairs of this life? This scripture states that this is just the starting place. No wonder there is so much chaos in the world.

The definition of wisdom from the Webster's New World Dictionary, is good judgement.

The standard of good judgement from the world view is much different than the kingdom perspective. In this world everything is relative but in the spiritual it's absolute.

With the Hebrews, truth and reality were synonymous. They meant the same thing. When our forefathers wrote the constitution, they had strong religious beliefs that the government should never interfere with the operation of the church. Now, in this day, many liberal thinkers have misinterpreted what they meant and call it "separation of church and state" for political purposes.

"For where you have envy and selfish ambition, there you find disorder and every evil practice. But the wisdom that comes from heaven is first of all pure, then peace-loving, considerate, submissive, full of mercy and good fruit, impartial and sincere." James 3:16-17

I believe this scripture draws a very clear contrast between the wisdom of God and that of the world. Let's look at another positive aspect of the fear of the Lord.

"The fear of the Lord is the beginning of knowledge, but fools despise wisdom and discipline." Proverbs 1"7

Knowledge comes from the Greek word 'ginosko' which means to know intimately and understand. Why have so many not sought this knowledge? Is it because so many other things in this life take precedence over it?

"This is what the Lord says. Let not the wise man boast of his wisdom or the strong man of his strength or the rich man boast of his riches, but let him who boast boast about this, that he understands and knows me, that I am the Lord who exercises kindness, justice and righteousness on earth, for in these I delight." Jeremiah 9:23-24

What could be better than knowing the Lord and His ways? This is the 'pearl of great price' that the kingdom of heaven is compared with. The parable said that when the man found it, he sold all he had and bought that field. Matthew 13:45-46

The more that I've gotten to know our sweet Jesus, the greater is my desire for intimacy. He's like a multifaceted diamond that has so many unique characteristics to it.

It's time to see where all of this is taking us in this great adventure.

"The Lord is exalted, for he dwells on high, he will fill Zion with justice and righteousness. He will be the sure foundation for your times, a rich store of salvation and wisdom and knowledge. The fear of the Lord is the key to this treasure." Isaiah 33:5-6

One thing that I know about a key, is that it unlocks something. I don't believe that it's our Heavenly Father's intention to keep anything from us but to preserve it for us.

It's time to embrace the 'fear of the Lord' and come into everything that God's called us to.

CHAPTER 12

The Sons of God

"We are the sons, the sons of God.
We do nothing of ourselves, but what the Father does.
The Father loves the sons and shows them what is done,
and that the world may marvel, He shows them things to
come.
We're the sons, the sons, the sons of God.
We are the sons, the sons, the sons of God.
As the Father raised the dead, so the sons shall too.
By the Spirit of the Father that lives in me and you.
By His Spirit we are to judge the living and the dead.
For we are the body,where Christ is the head.
In the beginning was the word and the word was God.
He came to His creation, but they received Him not.
He left a promise and a gift to confirm what He said.
That as many as received Him shall become the sons of
God."

(Vicki Parks)

In the beginning, the Heavenly Host created man in their image and likeness to have a godly offspring. It was God's original intention to have many after the prototype of Jesus Christ.

The fall interrupted his plan for several millenniums but God purposed to restore His man through the same medium that He used in the beginning.

"He was in the world, and the world was made by him, and the world knew him not. He came unto his own, and his own received him not. But as many as received him, to them gave he power to become the sons of God, even to them that believe on his name. Which were born, not of blood nor of the will of the flesh, nor of the will of man, but of God." John 1:10-13

Through our faith in Christ, God supernaturally births us into His family where there is neither male nor female. Since the fall, the human race has been searching for its identity and purpose for life. That's why Rick Warren's book, 'The Purpose Driven Life' is such a timely word. We are empty and unfulfilled until a connection with God is made.

"If you belong to Christ, then you are Abraham's seed and heirs according to the promise. What I'm saying is that as long as the heir is a child, he is no different from a slave, although he owns the whole estate. He's subject to guardians and trustees until the time set by his father. So, also, when we were children, we were in slavery under the basic principles of the world. But when the time had fully come, God sent his son, born of a woman, born under law, to redeem those under law, that we might receive the full rights of sons. Because you are sons, God sent the spirit of his son into our hearts, the spirit who calls out, Abba Father. So you are no longer a slave, but a son, and since you are a son, God has made you also an heir." Galatians 3:29-4:7

Relationally we've become the sons of God and positionally we are heirs of the new covenant. There's been a lot of teaching over the last thirty years concerning being in Christ. These speak of our identity in the Lord and what that means.

When Jesus was tempted by the devil in the desert, he disputed His identity when he stated, "If you are the son of God, tell these stones to become bread." Matthew 4:3

Our identity needs to be clearly established or we will be like the man in the book of James.

"Do not merely listen to the word, and so deceive yourselves. Do what it says. Anyone who listens to the word but does not do what it says is like a man who looks at his face in a mirror and, after looking at himself, goes away and immediately forgets what he looks like." James 1:22-24

I, personally went through this battle for my identity. My natural father, Walter Parks, was a professional engineer with the federal government. He climbed the civil service ladder to status of leadership.

I'd mentioned in another chapter, that I grew up as an overachiever. It didn't become apparent to me, what the root of this was, until I began to struggle with my relationship with God as my Heavenly Father.

Attempts were made to receive His love and affirmation but I was still uneasy about it. One day the Holy Spirit revealed to me, that I had a stronghold of rejection and believed that I had to earn His love.

This is why I strived so hard to earn my natural father's approval. The Holy Spirit led me into repentance and set me free from this stronghold.

It's very restraining to have a sense of disapproval and lack of acceptance. Many people deal with these issues, all of their lifes. I know through personal experience, the wonderful freedom that comes from the deliverance from wrong thinking.

Once our identity is firmly established, then we take our position as heirs. An heir is one who inherits the wealth and title of another. We are to carry on the legacy of our Heavenly Father.

There was a title that some Christians used several years ago, calling themselves, 'King's Kids'. They may have spoken it loosely but there is obvious truth to this statement of kinship.

The parable of the prodigal son best illustrates what a heir is. I won't write the whole parable but a few key verses.

"Jesus continued, there was a man who had two sons. The younger one said to his father, father give me my share of the estate. So he divided his property between them. My son, the father said, you are always with me, and everything I have is yours." Luke 15:11,12,31

The younger son obviously knew that he had an inheritance but didn't know how to steward it. The older son felt left out because of his misunderstanding of his inheritance.

Many who read the parable of the prodigal son, think that the main emphasis is forgiveness. That is definitely in the story but let me submit to you, that I believe 'sonship' was the cornerstone of it.

When the younger son returned, he didn't feel worthy to be called a son but the father affirmed him. Don't be too hard on these boys as we have all walked in their shoes.

"I pray also that the eyes of your heart may be enlightened in order that you may know the hope to which he has called you, the riches of his glorious inheritance in the saints." Ephesians 1:18

I love this scripture and think it would be good for us to pray it for one another. There's more for you and I to lay hold of in this life.

Have you considered that we are God's inheritance? He purchased us with Christ' blood. Isn't it great to be desired by him?

"In bringing many sons to glory, it was fitting that God, for whom and through whom everything exist, should make the author of their salvation perfect through suffering. Both the one who makes men holy and those who are made holy are of the same family. So Jesus is not ashamed to call them brothers." Hebrews 2:10-11.

God is gathering His people to Himself to display His glory. We are to participate in this family reunion with a complete understanding that we belong.

"I consider that our present sufferings are not worth comparing with the glory that will be revealed in us. The creation waits in eager expectation for the sons of God to be revealed." Romans 8:18-19

Things will be set in divine order when the sons of God rule and rein with Christ Jesus.

CHAPTER 13

A River of Life

There's a river of life that flows from my Throne,
flowing out by my Spirit.
A natural flow that's released to the earth,
bringing life wherever it goes.
A river of life,
springing up from my people.
Deposited there by my grace,
flowing out through their praise.
Let the living water, let it flow, flow naturally,
a well of life inside of you, let it flow, flow freely.
There's a river of life that flows from within,
springing up from your belly.
Release it, my children, in praise unto me,
it brings life wherever it goes."

(Vicki Parks)

The first mention of a river is the Genesis account of creation.

"Now the Lord God had planted a garden in the east, in Eden and there he put the man he had formed. And the Lord God made all kinds of trees grow out of the ground, trees that were pleasing to the eye and good for food. In the middle of the garden were the tree of life and the tree of the knowledge of good and evil. A river watering the garden flowed from Eden from there it was separated into four headwaters. The name of the first is the Pishon, it winds through the entire land of Havilah, where there is gold. The gold of that land is good, aromatic resin and onyx are also there. The name of the second river is the Gihon, it winds through the entire land of Cush. The name of the third river is the Tigris, it runs along the east side of Asshur. And the fourth river is the Euphrates." Genesis 2:8-14

From the Hebraic concept 'Eden' means pleasure. It was God's pleasure to place His man in a garden where He had easy access to him. God has always desired for man to be close to His heart. If you don't believe that, you'll have a difficult time understanding the gospel. That's what John 3:16 declares:

"For God so loved the world that he gave His one and only son, that whoever believes in Him shall not perish but have eternal life."

One of the rivers was called Pishon, which means fullness or abundance. God is always at maximum. Everything we need is in God's river. If you need healing or deliverance, it's in the river. If you need food, it's there. The river is the source of all life.

It was never God's intention that we suffer lack in anything but because of the fall, many people in our society do. When a person trust in Christ, they are reconnected to the river.

"Whoever believes in me as the scripture has said, streams of living water will flow from within him. By this He meant the Spirit whom those who believed in Him were later to receive. Up to that time the Spirit had not been given, since Jesus had not yet been glorified." John 7:38-39

A good friend of mine is always saying, God gives us the natural to learn the spiritual. In the scriptures, water is symbolic for the word of God and the Spirit of God.

God has provided His word and Spirit for every born again believer to partake of. It's sad that so many Christians live anemic lifes, void of power or victory.

Remember, Jesus had an encounter with a Samaritan woman concerning this.

"When a Samaritan woman came to draw water, Jesus said to her, will you give me a drink? His disciples had gone into the town to buy food. The Samaritan woman said to Him, you are a Jew and I am a Samaritan woman. How can you ask me for a drink?

For Jews do not associate with Samaritans. Jesus answered her, if you knew the gift of God and who it is that ask you for a drink, you would have asked Him and He would have given you living water. Sir, the woman said, you have nothing to draw with and the well is deep. Where can you get this living water?

Are you greater than our father Jacob, who gave us the well and drank from it himself, as did also his sons and his flocks and herds? Jesus answered, everyone who drinks this water will be thirsty again, but whoever drinks the water I give him will never thirst. Indeed, the water I give him will become in him a spring of water welling up to eternal life. The woman said to him, sir give me this water so that I won't get thirsty and have to keep coming here to draw water." John 4:7-15

Jesus used a common occurrence to reveal an eternal reality, that our greatest need isn't natural but spiritual. The people of this world are spiritually dead and live in the soulish realm. They feed off of the tree of the knowledge of good and evil and their senses are dull to the spiritual realm.

When, we are awakened unto righteousness and put our faith in Christ, new life is imparted. God's people have a life consciousness and begin to participate in the divine nature.

This delivers us from an orphan mentality, that we have to protect and provide for ourselves, freeing us up to serve God's eternal purpose.

"The man brought me back to the entrance of the temple, and I saw water coming out from under the threshold of the temple toward the east, for the temple face east. The water was coming down from under the south side of the temple, south of the altar. He then brought me out through the north gate and led me around the outside to the outer gate facing east, and the water was flowing from the south side.

As the man went eastward with a measuring line in his hand, he measured off a thousand cubits and then led me through water that was ankle deep. He measure off another thousand cubits and led me through water that was knee deep. He measured off another thousand and led me through water that was up to the waist. He measured another thousand, but now it was a river that I could not cross, because the water had risen and was deep enough to swim in, a river that no one could cross.

He asked me, son of man, do you see this? Then he led me back to the bank of the river. When I arrived there, I saw a great number of trees on each side of the river. He said to me, this water flows toward the eastern region and goes down into the Arabah, where it enters the sea. When it empties into the sea, the water there becomes fresh. Swarms of living creatures will live wherever the river flows. There will be large numbers of fish, because this water flows there and makes the salt water fresh, so where the river flows everything will live." Ezekiel 47:1-9

You can tell when a family is dysfunctional, marriages are separated, and churches divided, the river has stopped flowing and there's no life.

This was a vision given to the prophet Ezekiel depicting what God would do in the ages to come. The church has had many names for the different outpourings of God's Spirit; the Welch Revival, Pentecostal Movement, Latter Rain, and the Charismatic Renewal but I believe what's on the horizon is going to be so great that we'll just call it God.

The church will have a part to play in this final wave of God's Spirit. Let's return to the book of Genesis where we started this chapter and look at another river of significance.

Havilah means to bring forth fruit. When the church is truly moving in His Spirit, there will be life brought forth wherever we go. We'll find treasures in darkness and bring them to the light.

God promised never to destroy the earth again with a flood but He will bring it a river of life.

CHAPTER 14

Great is the Glory of the Lord

"I will praise thee with my whole heart,
before the Gods will I sing praise unto thee.
I will worship toward your holy temple,
and praise thy name for your kindness and truth.
For thou has magnified thy word above all thy name,
and great is the glory of the Lord.
Yea, I will sing in the ways of the Lord,
for great is the glory of the Lord.
In the day when I cry you answer me,
you strengthen me with strength in my soul.
All the kings of the earth shall praise thee, oh Lord,
when they hear the words of thy mouth.
Though I walk in the midst of trouble,
I know that thou wilt revive me, oh Lord.
You will stretch forth thy hand against mine enemies,
and thy right hand shall save me.
The Lord will perfect that which concerns me,
thy mercy, oh Lord is forever.
Forsake not the works of thine own hands,
for great is the glory of God."

(Vicki Parks)

Right after the Lord opened the Red Sea for the Israelites and drowned the Egyptians, Moses and Miriam led them in a song of praise to Him.

"Who among the gods is like you, o Lord? Who is like you, majestic in holiness, awesome in glory, working wonders? You stretched out your right hand and the earth swallowed them. In your unfailing love you will lead the people you have redeemed. In your strength you will guide them to your holy dwelling." Exodus 15:11-13

What a magnificent display of power and majesty this was, to deliver His people. In awe, all the Israelites could do, was to praise His greatness.

I read a really good teaching from the late David Wilkerson entitled "Right song on the wrong side". In this message, he brought out that the Israelites weren't exhibiting an ounce of faith in their song of praise just relief from the extreme situation.

They went through many hardships and trials in their trek into the desert. Praise was replaced with murmuring and complaining as they forgot their former deliverance.

Faith isn't a one act play but a life learning about the faithfulness of God. The Israelites had learned the ways of the Egyptians, to live based on circumstances of life and not to expect too much and hope for nothing.

Their leader, Moses, had his own concerns about leading this great nation to the promise land, flowing with milk and honey.

"Moses said to the Lord, you have been telling me, lead these people, but you have not let me know whom you will send with me. You have said, I know you by name and you have found favor with me. If you are pleased with me, teach me your ways so I may know you and continue to find favor with you.

Remember that this nation is your people. The Lord replied, my presence will go with you, and I will give you rest. Then Moses said to him, if your presence does not go with us, do not send us up from here. How will anyone know that you are pleased with me and with your people unless you go with us?

What else will distinguish me and your people from all the other people on the face of the earth? And the Lord said to Moses, I will do the very thing you have asked, because I am pleased with you and I know you by name. Then Moses said, now show me your glory." Exodus 33:12-18

God affirmed Moses, that He was pleased with him and would go with him to help lead His people. Moses was so stirred in his spirit, that he boldly demanded that the Lord reveal His glory to him. Have you ever been motivated like this, to want to know our God in the most intimate way?

This reminds me of a special encounter that I had with the Lord in the early eighties. Vicki and I were driving to San Angelo, Texas, when the Holy Spirit began to speak to me, in a very clear authoritative way. I'm so glad that I wasn't driving because I probably would have driven off the road.

He told me that I would be led into the school of Christ and be taught how to live in the Spirit. The Lord confirmed a prophetic call. After this episode, my life would never be the same.

I'm reminded of a powerful scripture on faith and how important it is to all of us.

"And without faith it is impossible to please God, because anyone who comes to him must believe that he exist and that he rewards those who earnestly seek him." Hebrews 11:6

What could be a greater reward than pleasing him and seeing his glory?

The children of Israel, like many today, don't care about relationship but only for their basic needs to be met.

Many, during Jesus time, missed their visitation and didn't see God in the flesh as foretold by the prophets.

"The son is the radiance of God's glory and the exact representation of his being, sustaining all things by his powerful word." Hebrews 1:3

This is why Jesus could tell his disciples, "Anyone who has seen me has seen the father." John 14:9

God, first revealed his glory to Israel, then Jesus manifest it to his disciples, and now the church is called to display the Lord's glory to the world.

"I consider that our present sufferings are not worth comparing with the glory that will be revealed in us." Romans 8:18

This takes an eternal perspective to see the reality of it. As I'm writing this, there are fires burning all over the state of Colorado. We're having a real bad one, here in Colorado Springs, where I live.

The people in the city are dismayed and don't know what to do. The city-wide church is praying and helping those in need, during this difficult time.

My local church gathered for a corporate prayer meeting, to pray for the fire to stop destroying homes. We sang a song that it would rain and that God would open the flood gates of heaven.

As we lifted up our voices, we could hear the rain coming down. Everyone spontaneously began to shout with joy.

This may sound like a coincidence to you but ever since I first believed in Jesus, I don't believe in them.

There has been a lot of discussion in recent years for the need of a paradigm shift. The world has had a victim mentality that things just happen to them. The church is to be more proactive than that.

When Jesus gave the great commission, He said that signs will accompany those who believe. These are supernatural manifestations of God's glorious power.

Again, the operative word is believe. The Holy Spirit spoke to me many years ago and said, "I'm limitless and want to be limitless in you."

Somehow, God's people have had a disconnect of how we're to participate in the divine nature by doing greater works than Christ. If we really believe that was God's plan, then maybe there would be more demonstrations of His miracle working power in the world today.

"The mystery that has been kept hidden for ages and generations, but is now disclosed to the saints. To them God has chosen to make known among the Gentiles the glorious riches of this mystery, which is Christ in you, the hope of glory." Colossians 1:26-27

Isn't it amazing, that the Lord of all creation has chosen you and me, the church, to be an important part of fulfilling His eternal purposes. Remember, Jesus said, "You did not choose me, but I chose you and appointed you to go and bear fruit, fruit that will last." John 15:16

Our part, as always, it to believe and obey. God will supply everything else by His grace and mighty power.

"For the earth will be filled with the knowledge of the glory of the Lord, as the waters cover the sea." Habakkuk 2:14

CHAPTER 15

The Unforced Rhythms of Grace

"Come unto me all ye that labor,
and I will give you rest.
Take my yoke, learn of me,
and you'll find rest for your soul.
For I am meek, and I am lowly,
my yoke is easy, my yoke is light.
Is not this the fast I have chosen,
to loose the bands of wickedness.
To undo the heavy burdens,
and let the oppressed go free.
Then shall thy light break forth as morning,
and your health will spring forth speedily.
My righteousness will go before thee,
and the glory of the Lord will be your reward.
Now deal thy bread to the hungry,
and bring the poor that are cast out to thy house.
When thou seest the naked, cover him,
and hide not thyself from from thine own flesh.
Then you shall call, and I will answer,
when you cry I'll say, here am I.
When you cease the speaking of vanities,
then the Lord will continually guide and satisfy."

(Vicki Parks)

"I have seen something else under the sun; the race is not to the swift or the battle to the strong, nor does food come to the wise or wealth to the brilliant or favor to the learned, but time and chance happen to them all." Ecclesiastes 9:11

I especially, want to consider the first part of this verse, concerning the race is not to the swift.

In high school, I ran cross country, which is approximately a two mile run. My coach worked diligently with me to build up my strength and endurance.

He told me that I probably wouldn't like him or the practices very much but it I would be faithful to do them, that I would be successful.

It was a good plan, for I became a strong runner. My attitude changed too and I became a tugboat instead of a showboat. When the actual races began, I beat boys that were faster than me but not in as good of shape as I was.

Some of the runners started the races fast but couldn't complete the course. I tried to pace myself and save enough energy to finish strong.

The Lord has revealed many things to me through this unique experience. Our lifes aren't a fifty yard dash but a marathon with much to learn along the way.

Listen to what the Apostle Paul had to say about this matter of running.

"Did you not know that in a race all the runners run, but only one gets the prize? Run in such a way as to get the prize. Everyone who competes in the games, goes into strict training. They do it to get a crown that will not last, but we do it to get a crown that will last forever.

Therefore I do not run like a man running aimlessly. I do not fight like a man beating the air. No, I beat my body and make it my slave so that after I have preached to others, I myself will not be disqualified for the prize." 1 Corinthians 9:24-27

Paul had similar ideas from his analogy of running to that of living the Christian life.

I just turned sixty old years old, last August, and it does cause you to stop and take inventory of your life. Being the reflective person that I am, it isn't hard to do.

God is so good, that He gave me the most wonderful helpmate in Vicki. She is so practical that she keeps this visionary's feet on the ground. Vicki has also, helped me to appreciate living in the moment, not always focused on point A to point B.

In the scripture, I just sighted, Paul stated that he didn't run like a man running aimlessly. This speaks of living purposely and not being side tracked. As the famous saying goes,"Aim at nothing and you're sure to hit it."

I take walks on the trails, behind my apartment, daily. It's my custom to go to an overhanging cliff and pray. One particular morning, I went there and a young man was seated and praying.

He heard me walk up and said hello. I asked him how he was doing and he told me that he was praying about going to a bible school in California.

The Holy Spirit impressed me to encourage him that this was a time of preparation for his calling and to really apply himself.

The wisdom, God gave Solomon, caused him to see the ebbs and flows of life and how unique they are.

"There is a time for everything and a season for every activity under heaven." Ecclesiastes 3:1 The word 'season' in Hebrew means 'appointed occasion' The Lord is setting up many divine appointments and training sessions for our growth and development.

Let's be encouraged with a latter verse in Ecclesiastes, chapter three, which speaks of his goodness.

"He has made everything beautiful in its time. He has also set eternity in the hearts of men, yet they cannot fathom what God has done from beginning to end." Ecclesiastes 3:11

It's of the upmost importance for us to see the beauty of whatever season that we're in or there'll be a misunderstanding of God's will and we'll find ourselves opposing it.

One of the marks of maturity isn't to be impetuous but to take things as they come. Another way to look at this, is, not trying to kick doors open but to wait on the Lord to open them.

Dr. Ed Cole wrote a very insightful book, many years ago, called 'Leaving and Entering.' He spoke of a right way to leave and a right way to enter.

The children of Israel didn't learn this lesson and it cost them, big time!

"Now Joseph and all his brothers and all that generation died, but the Israelites were fruitful and multiplied greatly and became exceedingly numerous, so that the land was filled with them.

Then a new king, who did not know about Joseph, came to power in Egypt. Look, he said to his people, the Israelites have become much too numerous for us. Come, we must deal shrewdly with them or they will become even more numerous and, if war breaks out, will join our enemies, fight against us and leave the country.

So they put slave masters over them to oppress them with force labor, and they built Pithom and Rameses as store cities for Pharaoh. But the more they were oppressed, the more they multiplied and spread, so the Egyptians came to dread the Israelites and worked them ruthlessly.

They made their lives bitter with hard labor in brick and mortar and with all kinds of work in the fields, in all their hard labor the Egyptians used them ruthlessly." Exodus 1:6-14

Joseph was second in command to Pharaoh and Jacob and his sons and their families moved to Egypt during the famine. They were all prospering and life was good until Joseph and his brothers and their generation died.

What was once a place of blessing turned into a fortress of bondage. They stayed too long and received the consequences of it.

That's why it's so important to be discerning of the times and seasons, to remain in step with the Lord. It's critical to know not only the will of God but His timing as well.

The definition of "Rhythm" is movement and flow. Vicki is always saying, "You need to go with the flow." To the Christian, this is living in the Spirit.

"So I say, live by the spirit and you will not gratify the desires of the sinful nature. For the sinful nature desires what is contrary to the spirit, and the spirit what is contrary to the sinful nature. They are in conflict with each other, so that you do not do what you want. But if you are led by the spirit, you are not under law." Galatians 5:16-18

If we've received the Holy Spirit, then we can move in a way of clear direction and resolve. He's not only our comforter but our guide.

There's another aspect of navigating through this matrix of life and that is this matter of grace.

"When the congregation was dismissed, many of the Jews and devout converts to Judaism followed Paul and Barnabas, who talked with them and urged them to continue in the grace of God." Acts 13:43

A balance of walking in the Spirit and being empowered by grace will help us to know God's will and timing.

This is "the unforced rhythms of grace."